YOU CAN SELL TO
UNCLE SAM

YOU CAN SELL TO
UNCLE SAM

GETTING GOVERNMENT CONTRACTS

Cal Stevens

www.tacadamarketing.com

YOU CAN SELL TO UNCLE SAM
GETTING GOVERNMENT CONTRACTS

iUniverse books may be ordered through booksellers or by contacting:

iUniverse
1663 Liberty Drive
Bloomington, IN 47403
www.iuniverse.com
1-800-Authors (1-800-288-4677)

ISBN: 978-1-4917-5135-0 (sc)
ISBN: 978-1-4917-5136-7 (e)

Printed in the United States of America.

iUniverse rev. date: 12/04/2014

Table of Contents

Foreword

It takes tenacity to succeed in government sales or to sell your products or services to "Uncle Sam." Establishing a small business in the federal marketplace can be frustrating. Yet, small business preference programs, along with knowledge of how procurements are conducted, can cause small business revenues to increase in a few short years performing on government contracts. This book will provide guidance on how your company can position itself in selling its products or services to Uncle Sam.

I wish to thank the following who made this book possible: God, for guiding me in this long journey; my wife, Eleanor, who encouraged me to finish the manuscript which started soon after I retired from GSA in 2009; my children-- David, Calvin, Jr., and Tammie (an author in her own right); and my three grandchildren--Terry, Rosi, and Raven. Special thanks to Diane Adams who edited and assisted me in putting the final touches on the manuscript.

Calvin Stevens, President
TACADA Marketing Consultants, LLC

Introduction

It takes tenacity to succeed in government sales or to sell your products or services to "Uncle Sam." Establishing a small business in the federal marketplace can be frustrating. Yet small business preference programs, and general knowledge of the procurement process, can cause a small business to grow or increase revenues in a few short years if it has what Uncle Sam needs.

If you have considered or researched entering the government marketplace recently, you can't help but notice the popularity of General Services Administration (GSA) Federal Supply Schedule (FSS) or Multiple Award Schedule (MAS) contracts. The general consensus is -- small businesses need a GSA Schedule to be competitive. For the most part, military procurement agents will not consider businesses that do not hold a GSA contract.

Uncle Sam spent more than $385 billion in contract dollars during Fiscal Year 2013. The GSA Schedule program (from this point on, I will use Federal Supply Schedule--FSS or Multiple Award Schedule--MAS Program interchangeably), for example, is a vital procurement tool for civilian and military agencies, as well as a potential source of nearly limitless revenue for GSA Schedule vendors. That means YOU! However, winning a Schedule award can be a complex, time-consuming, and costly process and, to be honest, it simply isn't the right fit for some businesses.

Did you know that, according to the U.S. Small Business Administration, small businesses employ about half of American workers and account for approximately 65% of new jobs created? Given the importance of small businesses, the government has established programs to assist them with getting their fair share of federal contracting dollars. The current goal is for 23% of the money from federal contracts to be awarded to small businesses. As a sub-goal, the federal government aims to award five percent of federal contracting dollars to women; five percent to small, disadvantaged businesses; three percent to service disabled veterans; and three percent to firms located in a HUBZone.

This book offers a comprehensive overview of what you need to do to prepare for procurement opportunities, the types of schedules, and the award process. It focuses on specific information useful for determining if getting a GSA Schedule is the right decision for your company, and if so, how to meet requirements for obtaining an award more quickly.

What are GSA Schedules or contracts? You may have heard the term "GSA Number" or "Schedule Contract." A GSA Multiple Award Schedule (MAS) is a pre-approved contract to do business with Uncle Sam. Becoming a GSA Schedule holder deems you worthy of federal business; your prices have been determined to be fair and reasonable and, finally, your competency in your field has been given a stamp of approval. Government buyers know you are not a risky prospect and can make purchases from you directly through GSA Advantage!®, (the government's online shopping mall), or with any government purchase card (GSA contracts permit the use of government credit card purchases).

The GSA Multiple Award Schedule (MAS) or Federal Supply Schedule (FSS) program is the premier commercial acquisition vehicle program within the Federal Government. There are currently 41 different schedules that are multiple award, indefinite delivery, indefinite quantity (IDIQ) contracts for commercial products and services that are available for use by federal agencies worldwide. GSA awards and administers MAS contracts pursuant to 40 United States Code (U.S.C.) 501, Services for Executive Agencies, and 41 U.S.C. 259, which references GSA's MAS program.

A GSA Schedule contract is attractive to both buyer and seller; it's a win - win situation. Remember, billions of dollars are spent each fiscal year through GSA contracts by civilian and military agencies. Now is the time for you to get your share of the billions of federal procurement dollars.

Let's briefly look at some of the reasons small businesses do not submit bids or solicitations for government contracts.

1. Sources reveal that only five percent of bids without pre-marketing result in contract awards. Many small firms do not have the resources or expertise to submit quality bids.

2. Eighty percent of all federal government bidders lose about 70% percent of the opportunities on which they bid. Again, many small firms do not have the knowledge to understand the procurement process. They just give up seeking federal procurement opportunities.

3. Out of an estimated 413,000 firms registered in System for Award Management (SAM), formerly Central Contractor Registration (CCR), many large firms receive almost 50% of federal contract dollars as reported in **Government Executive Magazine**. More information will be provided on SAM and the registration process later.

This book will provide guidance on how your company can position itself in selling its products or services to Uncle Sam. There are probably thousands of books on how to sell to the Federal Government, (a.k.a, Uncle Sam), how to market to the Federal Government, and above all, how to obtain a government contract. What makes this book different from all others on selling to the government is the knowledge I've gained in over 30 years in various capacities with GSA – Administrative Contracting Officer, Travel and Transportation Director, Marketing Specialist, Warehouse Distribution Manager, and Quality Assurance Specialist. Each position prepared me on the internal workings of how the government, specifically GSA, solicits or bids for products or services. These positions also prepared me to know how Uncle Sam (again, GSA) procures, administers, markets, and operates in dealing with small businesses. For the past 15 years, I've traveled across this great country conducting numerous outreach seminars and workshops to the business community offering tips and strategies on how to succeed in government marketing and procurement. As a result, I feel a pressing need to continue my efforts to provide this same quality service as a consultant, to assist small business on how to obtain government contracts, and how to market its products and services to Uncle Sam.

By writing this book, I am fulfilling a life-long dream of giving back to the business community. I am very much interested in knowing how this book and its process assisted your efforts in obtaining a GSA schedule contract. Please submit your comments to:

TACADA Marketing Consultants
Attn: "Comments on Book"
P.O. Box 373855
Decatur, GA 30037-3855

You may also email your comments to: president@tacadamarketing.com. In the Subject line, please write: "Comments on Book."

I appreciate you buying this book, and I appreciate and welcome your comments. Thanks, and may God's blessings be forever with you in all your endeavors!

Chapter One – First Things First

One of the first requirements in submitting your solicitation is to consider these three very important questions:

1. Which government agency buys my products or services?
2. How do I get in touch with them?
3. How do I market to them?

I will attempt, based on my prior experience with General Services Administration (GSA), to provide a brief overview of the procurement process and to offer tips and strategies for successful submission of your pending solicitation.

If you are ready, let's get started. First of all, Uncle Sam buys information technology, office supplies, hand tools, etc. In order to determine what Uncle Sam buys, you need to research each agency's website. Uncle Sam is the largest purchaser of products and services in the world, and is projected to spend over $400 billion in fiscal year 2014 and beyond. The Federal Government should be your number one customer and, if you are serious about making this happen, you must have a GSA contract.

One very important website you need to be familiar with is www. gsa.gov. Once you log onto this website, click on the left side of the homepage, "For Business," then click on "Getting on Schedule." This "For Vendors - Getting on Schedule" link has a wealth of information for you to get started in determining if you are really serious and want to learn more about doing business with Uncle Sam.

There are other websites I strongly encourage you to visit during your initial search. These websites can be found if you log onto: www.USA.gov. Click on "For Businesses and Nonprofits" at the top of this homepage.

Then click on "Sell to the Government." Another powerful website to visit is the U.S. Government Manual:

www.gpoaccess.gov/manual. This website has hundreds of helpful tips on doing business with Uncle Sam. I highly recommended you click on the various links on the left side of the home page to learn further information and receive guidance with your research efforts.

You also need to target one to three agencies you want to do business with. Often, businesses seeking government contracts want to target every federal and military agency, or Uncle Sam, in general. I am not saying you can't target every agency if you have the resources which include time, money and effort. What I'm saying is, narrow your search down to two or three agencies you definitely want to target based on your scope of work. The key words are "scope of work." You don't want to target the Department of Homeland Security (DHS) if you are selling golf balls. Then again, perhaps some top senior official within DHS may "need" a box of golf balls. Notice I said "need" rather than "want." You also have to determine what is essential to that particular agency.

Another determining factor is your search of available websites. Here is a website, operated by GSA, you need to consider. It is the main portal if you are seeking procurement opportunities. From this moment on, you should be familiar with www.fedbizopps.gov. This website was established to post all procurement opportunities over $25,000.

From this website, you will be able to locate a forecast of procurement or contracting opportunities from every federal agency with links to the Subcontracting Directory, "Sub-Net," and Business Partner Network (BPN).

Here are some helpful tips on accessing Federal Business Opportunities (FedBizOpps):

Let's go to: www.fedbizopps.gov.

Click on FedBizOpps Vendors. FedBizOpps provides easy access 24 hours per day, 7 days a week, to:

- Synopses/Pre-Solicitation Notices,
- Solicitations/Requests for Proposals or Quotes,
- Federal Acquisition Regulations (click on link to ACQNET Home Page on FedBizOpps.),

- Market Surveys/Sources Sought,
- Amendments/Modifications/Awards (Subcontracting Opportunities).

As previously mentioned, various federal agencies and military services post contracting opportunities or solicitations over $25,000 on FedBizOpps. The number of participating agencies continues to increase. In the future, FedBizOpps will expand to include electronic receipt of bids, proposals, and quotes. Uncle Sam, or the Federal Government, is using FedBizOpps to work toward a paperless form of procurement.

GSA and other agencies post their major procurement opportunities, including the Multiple Award Schedule (MAS) contracts, on FedBizOpps. Multiple Award Schedule (MAS) solicitations are continuously open with no bid opening or bid closing date. So, if you are interested in seeking procurement opportunities with GSA or any other federal agency, go to FedBizOpps. Here is how potential vendors can search for contracting opportunities:

- Click on selected bidding document or choose appropriate Classification Code.
- Select Offices and Locations of federal agencies or the military.
- Watch for current procurements by Posted Dates.
- Check on Award data to identify subcontracting opportunities.

Classification Code:

- Click on the Classification Code of the agency (listed in the matrix) you want to search.
- Scroll down listing of business opportunities watching for two-digit product codes or alphabetical service codes.
- Click on Procurements for the products and services your company provides.

Search by Solicitation Number:

- Click on Find Business Opportunities. Enter the solicitation number and click on Start Search.
- Click on Solicitation, Sol, or Sols, and click on Solicitation.

- Choose from the matrix how you want to access the bidding document (Zip Compressed Files or Microsoft Word).
- Print the solicitation directly from the screen or save to the hard drive and print from there.

Vendor Notification Service (Online Bidders Mailing List Application):

- Click on Vendor Notification Service, choose 1, 2 or 3 (No. 2 is recommended); then, enter your e-mail address.
- Choose the appropriate Classification Code(s) – for more than one code, hold down the Control Key and click on each number or letter applicable.
- Choose the agency or agencies for notification of their postings by clicking on "All Agencies," clicking on one agency or holding down the Control Key and clicking on each agency selected.
- Click on Subscribe to Mailing List to register.
- To update your information, click on Unsubscribe, type in your e-mail address, and enter your registration again.

If you are a veteran-owned small business, here is one particular website I encourage you to visit and register for further procurement opportunities: VETS GWAC (Veterans Government Wide Acquisition Contract) or www. vetbiz.gov. Questions on VETS GWAC may be submitted to vetsgwac@gsa.gov or by calling the Small Business GWAC Center, toll free, at (877) 327-8732.

Here is some additional information for veterans unveiled by the U.S. Department of Transportation and the U.S. Department of Veterans Affairs. These websites are designed to help military veterans find jobs and other opportunities in the transportation industry. The portals are available at www.dot.gov and www.va.gov.

Here are some additional legislative laws for veterans:

- Public Law (P. L.) 108-183, the Veteran's Benefits Act of 2003, was signed in December 2003.
- Section 308 of P. L. 108-183, "Procurement Program for Small Business Concerns Owned and Controlled by Service-Disabled

Veterans," provides for set-aside and sole source procurement authority for service-disabled veteran-owned small business (SDVOSB) concerns.

- Executive Order 13360 directs that at least three percent of all federal agencies' contracting dollars go to businesses owned by service-disabled veterans.
- GSA signed an agreement with VET-Force, the Task Force for Veteran's Entrepreneurship, to help increase GSA's efforts to spend three percent of its contracting dollars on companies owned by service-disabled veterans.

GSA and VET-Force will work together to increase internal and external awareness of the capabilities of businesses owned by service-disabled veterans, and it will provide appropriate training to both federal contracting staffs and service-disabled veteran businesses.

The agreement supports an Executive Order directing agencies to increase contracting with businesses owned by service-disabled veterans, also known as SDVOSBs, (service-disabled veteran-owned small businesses). GSA established an initiative-- the 21 Gun Salute-- to help reach the agency's three percent goal. This agreement with VET-Force is part of the initiative. For more information, call (202) 501-1231.

Finally, In order to fully understand the process involved in "Getting on Schedule," I recommend you visit this website for vendors or potential vendors and take the Center for Acquisition Excellence online, self-paced training course, "Pathway to Success." The course describes:

- Various features of the GSA Schedules Program,
- How to submit an offer,
- The evaluation and contract award process,
- How to successfully market supplies and services, and
- Sources of information related to Schedule contract administration.

FedConnect:

The FedConnect® product is a centralized marketplace, hosted by Compusearch, where individuals and organizations can find and pursue funding opportunities.

Organizations seeking grants and funding can search opportunities and submit applications directly through FedConnect. FedConnect will even notify the organizations of new funding opportunities as they are posted. Once the agency makes the award it can be delivered through FedConnect, and all post-award activity and communication can also be managed through FedConnect. For more information about FedConnect, log onto: www.fedconnect.net.

End Notes

Chapter Two – Your Homework Assignment

In this chapter you will be given an opportunity to do some homework. After researching the various website(s) on FedBizOpps and other procurement websites, start developing your strategy on how you plan to analyze, write, develop, and submit your solicitation. I warn you, this process takes time. However, this time is well-spent if you really plan to succeed in government procurement.

The first requirement for your business is to register (if you have not already done so) on these websites:

- Obtain a Dun & Bradstreet Number (DUNS Number) if you don't already have one. (See http://www.dnb.com/US/duns_update/index.html).
- Register at The System for Award Management (SAM), formerly Central Contractor Registry. SAM's registration site: http://www.sam.gov/.

What is SAM? The System for Award Management (SAM) has combined and completed the federal procurement systems and the **Catalog of Federal Domestic Assistance** into one new system. The final phase of SAM includes the functionality from the following systems:

- Central Contractor Registry (CCR),
- Federal Agency Registration (FedReg),
- Online Representations and Certifications Application,
- Excluded Parties List System (EPLS).

How will SAM benefit me?

The overarching benefits of SAM include streamlined and integrated processes, elimination of data redundancies, and reduced costs while providing improved capability. More importantly, you must be registered in this database if you wish to get paid! Enough said? NOTE: There are over 430,000 companies registered in SAM. However, there are less than 10,000 companies with GSA contracts!

- Register at the Online Representations and Certifications Application (ORCA) site. (See https://orca.bpn.gov/login.aspx).
- Sign up to receive emails about federal opportunities at the central Federal Business Opportunities site. Go to http://www.fedbizopps.gov. The "FedBiz Now" subscription service is a superior way to receive federal business opportunities. You can subscribe at: http://www.fedmarket.com/products/product-fbn.shtml (please go back and review Chapter One).

The second requirement is to determine what Uncle Sam buys. Important questions you need to consider are: Can I fulfill this requirement or scope of work? Can I make a profit? (Now that is a statement in itself!). Why in the world would I mention "profit" at this point in determining if you want to sell to Uncle Sam? Remember, many agencies, like GSA, are self-sustaining or operate under the Industrial Funding Fee (IFF) Concept. These agencies with IFF do not, for the most part, receive appropriated funding from Congress, and must receive funding through the use of schedules and other funding resources. That's where GSA receives a portion of all sales as a result of your company being awarded a multiple award schedule contract. Currently, the IFF is 0.75% of all sales payable to GSA each quarter. Years ago, the IFF was 1.0% of sales. Congress has been trying to further reduce this IFF to 0.5% of sales. I'm not sure if there are any initiatives in Congress to further reduce this fee. So, in the meantime, businesses will have to comply with contract terms in reporting the 0.75% to GSA on a quarterly basis.

In determining how to price your product or service, you must take into consideration the IFF to establish your hourly rate or how to price the product you plan to submit during the solicitation process and, ultimately, sell to Uncle Sam. Remember, we are talking about Schedule contract sales!

Once you determine your target, you definitely need to determine the scope of work. How can your company position itself in providing a quality product or service under the terms and conditions of the solicitation? Now, you are ready to actually download the solicitation. The scope of work tells exactly what Uncle Sam needs. A written proposal is often the first time an agency hears about your business. To make that first impression a good one, and more importantly, to make certain you follow applicable federal regulations and other directives, here are a few basic rules to follow:

Tip Number 1: Read the RFP or RFQ <u>very</u> carefully.

A proposal or solicitation is often written in response to a published RFP (Request for Proposal) or RFQ (Request for Quote). These are documents outlining, in varying levels of detail, the goods to be purchased or services to be contracted. They also give strong indications of the primary focus areas by the administration of the agency or management of the corporation. You will be wise to respond to these focus areas specifically and with some attention to detail.

Tip Number 2: Undertake the basic research.

Basic research for proposal writing can take many forms, but the principal areas in which to concentrate your efforts are: (a) understanding the contracting agency or corporation, and (b) the competition. You can learn amazing amounts of information about the vendor by researching past RFP's and finding out who responded-- and-- who won those bids. Usually, initial research takes the form of a simple phone call to find out how much of this information is available and where to get it. The Internet has made everyone's job easier, and it pays to use the Net to track down not only vendor information, but also more data on possible competition. Other resources include industry trade magazines and discussions with professional organizations. In tracking down possible competitors, use simple filters in your search such as geographic guidelines and industry experience requirements stipulated in the RFP. Unless you have a strategic reason to do otherwise, for the short-term goal of writing your proposal, there is little sense in tracking down competitors who do not qualify for the current or past RFP's.

Tip Number 3: Keep your proposal simple and to the point.

Your proposal should address the specific questions and focus areas of the RFP. Use very simple language that clearly spells out what your company intends to do to fulfill the bid. Show supporting detail and references where asked, and clearly state how you intend to solve the problems specifically addressed by the RFP. Do not assume that the reader of your proposal has extensive industry experience. And, when asked to present pricing, use numbers that will ensure your firm makes a profit from this contract. Above all, sell the capabilities of your business in clear and concise language, and use exact supporting information to help state your case on why your firm is the best one for the job. Very often, the RFP will call for past performance as part of the RFP, so it pays to stay in touch with previous contracting officers with whom your company performed. It is also a good idea to get testimonials from them to include in your past performance package.

Tip Number 4: Follow the presentation guidelines.

The RFP usually has clear guidelines on how your proposal should be presented or packaged. These guidelines include the number of narrative pages, font size, spacing, and an index of forms to be completed. They may also include presentation parameters such as binding (or no binding), cover information, labels, and overall packaging. One other obstacle--most RFP's can be modified at any time by the issuing vendor. Governmental agencies will require that you comply with any amendments or modifications to an RFP, even those issued a few days before the proposal due date. You must continually monitor the website or other information center that handles the RFP to ensure that no such amendment has been issued. In addition, your completed proposal generally requires the amended or modified RFP pages to be signed and attached as part of your response and package.

Here is a very important point to consider. Several years ago, GSA changed its solicitation process and made it mandatory that ALL solicitations be submitted electronically! No hard copy solicitations will be accepted. This means your company must seek approval and verification to use an electronic digital signature to sign all documents relative to your solicitation.

Tip Number 5: Consider getting help with the proposal process.

The proposal writing and respondent process is as much an art as it is a science. If you, or your firm, have never been involved in that process, it can be daunting. If possible, try to obtain copies of past proposals written by firms like yours, (with the owner's permission), to see how an RFP was crafted. If you are serious about the process, the best money you may spend will be in retaining a professional writer of proposals and grants. Not only will they bring their writing capabilities to the process, they will bring an independent viewpoint to your business and its capabilities. Another possibility is to seek assistance from a local Procurement Assistant Center or PTAC (see Chapter Six for website). This organization was established to provide guidance to small businesses seeking government procurement.

Tip Number 6: Complete requirements for Opening Ratings (or past performance evaluation).

What, exactly, is an Opening Ratings evaluation or report? The Past Performance Evaluation (PPE) report provides a robust and independent view of supplier past performance by leveraging survey feedback from a supplier's customers, together with business intelligence and analytical expertise, powered by Opening Ratings, a division of Dun & Bradstreet (D&B.) The report assesses supplier performance relative to peers in the same industry and is often requested as part of a vendor bid process. For more information, go to: www.ppereports.com. It is a mandatory requirement in all GSA solicitations, and you may order reports directly from Opening Ratings. Instructions can be found in each GSA solicitation.

It has been said, "If you fail to plan, you plan to fail!" In this chapter, it is your responsibility to perform due diligence in order to become successful in your quest to become a government contractor.

End Notes:

Chapter Three –
Develop a Marketing Strategic Plan

According to data compiled by Eagle Eye Publishers, Inc., federal spending with small businesses increased by more than $10 billion from fiscal year 2007 to 2008. But, the 12 percent jump lags behind the total federal procurement spending increase of 18 percent. While small business contracts are on the rise, these firms are capturing a smaller piece of the pie at a time when spending is ballooning. Since the recession of 2008 and reduced government spending, many federal agencies have seen a slight increase in spending. According to the latest **2013 Annual Review of Government Contracting,** by the National Contract Administration and Bloomberg Federal, spending on MAC (Multiple Award Contracts) increased by 21 percent in fiscal year 2013, up approximately 20 percent over fiscal year 2012. This increase is remarkable considering the total federal spending decline over the past five years.

It is important to develop a marketing strategy to plan for success in providing supplies and services to Uncle Sam.

Marketing Strategy: Tips for Developing a Marketing Strategy:

- Getting Started
    - Research, Research, Research. Look at agency budgets, missions and goals.
    - Identify problems you can solve (one source is IG Reports).
    - Identify specific agencies/customers to target.
    - Identify size and scope of opportunities to pursue.

- Next
  - Relationships, Relationships, Relationships: Make contact with procurement, technical, and program personnel.
  - Pursue opportunities (surf the Web).
  - Build your own opportunity/customer database.
- Maximize Web Presence

Once you have been awarded a GSA Schedule Contract:

  - Provide customers with a web address that sends them directly to your GSA contract info. Include the GSA Starmark on your homepage.
  - Get on GSA Advantage!®. Provide quality descriptions and pictures, use all key words, keep information updated.
  - Include a link to your homepage.
  - Review e-Buy daily.

Sales and Marketing S.W.O.T.—A new use for a traditional tool

The S.W.O.T. Analysis, where you evaluate your **S**trengths, **W**eaknesses, **O**pportunities, and **T**hreats, is well-known in the business planning process. Many companies use this method during strategic planning exercises as a way to form strategies and make decisions on new business ventures or initiatives. It is powerful, because it looks at both internal (strengths, weaknesses) and external (opportunities, threats) forces.

As powerful as the S.W.O.T. Analysis is for business planning, it is equally powerful in sales and marketing decision-making. By employing this traditional tool to each of your sales and marketing activities, you can take advantage of your strengths, uncover new opportunities, minimize your weaknesses, and eliminate your threats in amazing ways. However, that is only if you can be objective. Otherwise, the exercise falls flat.

While the S.W.O.T. Analysis can be applied to decisions about business planning, product development and other strategic decision-making tasks, consider using it for the following two sales and marketing activities:

- **Deciding on Marketing Vehicles.** Use the S.W.O.T. Analysis to evaluate each marketing vehicle in your marketing plan. This will allow you to focus marketing efforts on the vehicles where you have the most advantage or opportunity and the least amount of weakness or threat.
- **Developing Sales Presentation/Proposals.** Apply the S.W.O.T. Analysis to the development of each of your sales presentations and proposals. Be sure to focus the analysis on evaluating each section based on issues specific to the customer you are pitching.

As you approach your S.W.O.T. Analysis, consider the following questions:

- **Strengths:** What advantages does your company/product have that no one else has? What makes you unique? Focus on those things that make your offer compelling to a prospect or customer.
- **Weaknesses:** Where can you improve? Where have you made mistakes in the past? What do you not have that other companies/ products in your industry have? Focus on those things that detract from your offer.
- **Opportunities:** What trends lend to your strengths? What is the "expansion" potential over time? Opportunities are external factors that represent why your company exists or should/can grow.
- **Threats:** What challenges do you face? What are your competitors doing? What is the overall competitive landscape? Threats-- such as competition, operational capacity, cost of goods increases, etc., are external forces that could impact your success.

No matter the purpose, using the S.W.O.T. Analysis can force thoughtful, strategic, and creative thinking. When used properly, the S.W.O.T. Analysis not only helps you identify your strengths, weaknesses, opportunities, and threats, it also helps you determine your strategies for addressing each one.

What is an SMS (Successful Marketing Strategy)?

Uncle Sam wants you to be successful, and Uncle Sam will assist you in every way legally possible. But, just as you market your commercial business, you must market your business to government customers. However, your marketing strategy is quite different from that used to market your commercial business because of the multiple of oversights (Congress, GAO, FAR, and other regulations) associated with government procurements. Establishing a marketing strategy at the outset will help you reach your target audience. The following section will assist you in creating a successful marketing strategy. Remember, this strategy is also helpful for your company even if you don't seek government contracts.

Where to Start?

First, understand your company's value position; i.e., what you can do to help solve an agency's problem. Consider what value your product or service brings to the customer.

To get a better handle on your value position, ask these questions:

- What does your organization do?
- Who, in the government, has a requirement for your product or service?
- How does your company help the government meet its goals and objectives?
- Provide examples of customers your organization has assisted in the past and the corresponding results.
- What appeal does your product or services have that caused customers to use you in the past?

After understanding your value position:

- Evaluate why the agency would buy your product or services.
- Get information on their budgets and look at their mission and goals.

It is also helpful to look at Government Accountability Office (GAO) Reports. To find copies of GAO Reports, go to: http://www.gpoaccess.gov/gaoreports/index.html.

Get the agency's organization chart and then develop a call plan.

Maximize your CWP (Company's Web Presence).

Make sure you provide the web address that sends the customer directly to your GSA contract information. Also, if you have a company website established, consider providing links through GSA Advantage!® directly to your home page. There are some restrictions, but this is an excellent way to avoid a duplication of efforts and "wow" your customers with all the services you have available. It's your contract. Make the most of it. Additionally, remember to load your company's information to GSA Advantage!®. If 'you're not on GSA Advantage!®, you're not going to be visible to the agencies.

Next, make sure your company does the following:

- Target the size and scope of agency opportunities to be pursued within the next 12-18-24 months.
- Construct a database in which to track federal opportunities including supplemental information (i.e., names, addresses, and phone numbers of agency contacts and procurement personnel).
- Prepare additional print and online materials marketing your company. Please use the GSA Starmark to promote your company's benefit of being on a GSA Schedule. Electronic downloads are available at: http://apps.fss.gsa.gov/partnership/logos.cfm.
- Obtain copies of expiring contracts, if possible.
- Contact procurement, technical, and program manager personnel in order to build relationships.
- Attend workshops to further develop presentation skills, to better understand the federal purchasing processes, and to improve your proposal preparation skills.
- Look for Inspector General Reports that identify problems your company can solve.
- Learn about the Agency's budget and how much money they have going into various functional areas.

When an opportunity presents itself:

- Understand your organization's value relative to the opportunity; i.e., can you do it yourself or should you team with or fill a gap with a partner(s) who would help you beat other team solutions?
- Does your team uniquely solve the government's problem?
- Is it the right job for your company?
- Does your past performance give the customer confidence you can do the job?
- Understand what risks are involved and how they would be mitigated.
- Develop a competitive matrix and rank yourself against others who are bidding.
- Question your solution to ensure it is truly the best.

A well-developed marketing strategy goes a long way toward highlighting your company's past performance history, its scope of work objectives and, above all, its ability to provide a much needed quality product or service so Uncle Sam can meet or exceed its mission.

(Author's Note: This last tip or marketing strategic should be used once you are awarded a GSA schedule contract).

End Notes:

Chapter Four –
Implementing Your Tactical Plans

The Evaluation Process

To help you better understand the meaning of key solicitation terms and conditions, and to help you understand the evaluation process, here are some helpful tips and strategies you need to consider:

The evaluation process is where the "rubber meets the road." Here you are required to provide information about yourself, your company, and how you plan to proceed under the terms and conditions of the contract.

Federal Acquisition Regulation (FAR) 16.501-1 defines an indefinite delivery contract as a "Delivery Order Contract." That means a contract for supplies that does not procure or specify a firm quantity of supplies (other than a minimum or maximum quantity), and that provides for the issuance of orders for the delivery of supplies during the period of the contract.

"Task Order Contract" means a contract for a service(s) that does not procure or specify a firm quantity of services (other than a minimum or maximum quantity), and that provides for the issuance of orders for the performance of tasks during the period of the contract.

Once your solicitation is received, the Procuring Contracting Officer (PCO) determines the following:

- **Responsiveness**
    - Read all documents in their entirety.
    - Fill them in completely.
    - Leave no blanks filled in with "N/A".

- **Responsibility**
  - Viable product/service
  - History of satisfactory performance
  - Financial resources
- **Fair and Reasonable Pricing**

Here is a sample descriptive section of Schedule70--General Purpose Commercial Information Technology Equipment, Software, and Services Solicitation:

- Type: Solicitation
- Posted Date: April 30, 2014
- Description: 01 - Read Me First
- Description: 02 - Solicitation
- Description: 03 - SF1449
- Description: 04 - Regulations Incorporated by Reference
- Description: 05 - Past Performance Evaluation
- Description: 06 - Small Business Sub-contracting Plan
- Description: 07 - Proposal Price List Preparation
- Description: 08 - Commercial Sales Practice Format (CSP-1)
- Description: 09 - Agent Authorization Letter
- Description: 10 - Letter of Supply Template
- Description: 11 - SCA Wage of Determinations Index
- Description: 12 - Sample Labor Category Matrix
- Description: 13 - Critical Information Specific to Schedule 70

In every GSA solicitation there is a document or attachment which says, "Read Me First." I strongly encourage you to read and re-read this information prior to submitting your solicitation. It is important that you read and follow instructions, or you will be considered non-responsive.

READ ME FIRST:

Under the Multiple Award Schedule (MAS) or Federal Supply Schedule (FSS) Program, the General Services Administration and the Department of Veterans Affairs (GSA/VA) establish long-term government-wide contracts with commercial firms to provide ordering activities with access to a wide variety of commercial supplies and/or services. This information provides pertinent background information on the FSS Program. You should consider this information prior to deciding whether to submit an offer for an FSS contract. Please read this "Read Me First" in its entirety to learn about the benefits and responsibilities associated with being an FSS contractor. You will then be better informed to determine if obtaining a multiple award contract (FSS) is the right business decision for your firm. *AUTHOR'S NOTE: I will be using the term, FSS Program, which is the same as the Multiple Award Schedule Program (MAS).*

The FSS Program is designed to enable ordering activities to purchase commercial supplies and/or services quickly, efficiently, at fair and reasonable prices, and still meet all the requirements of the Federal Acquisition Regulation (FAR). The commercial supplies and/or services awarded under FSS contracts are divided into approximately 41 distinct schedules. In total, there are approximately 20,000 FSS contracts in place with more added daily, covering over 11 million supplies and/or services.

To assist suppliers, GSA designed the Vendor Toolbox, which can be found in the Vendor Education Center https://gsafas.secure.force.com/MASTrainingHome). The Vendor Toolbox walks the supplier through researching, analyzing, and deciding whether it is the best business decision to pursue a GSA Schedule contract. If the supplier decides to become an offeror, it provides an understanding of the steps needed to be successful in the federal marketplace. In addition to the direct link to the Vendor Education Center, prospective suppliers can reach the two main components of the Vendor Toolbox, Pathway to Success, and the Readiness Assessment, under the "Education" tab on the Vendor Support Center (https://vsc.gsa.gov). Please note the Vendor Toolbox training can only be completed using a Windows based computer with an Internet Explorer or Firefox browser.

1. AbilityOne Program:

The AbilityOne Program is a federal procurement program that generates jobs for individuals who are blind or have another significant disability through the manufacturing of products or the provision of services required by federal personnel. Products and services on the AbilityOne Procurement List are mandatory for use by federal customers. The mandatory source requirement of the AbilityOne Program, as outlined by the Javits-Wagner-O'Day (JWOD) Act (41 U.S.C. 46 – 48c), must be adhered to by all schedule holders. Certain commercial products are considered "essentially the same" (ETS) as AbilityOne products. Because the AbilityOne products are mandatory purchases for federal customers, contractors are required to remove the commercial ETS items from their offer. If you offer products that are ETS as AbilityOne products, you are encouraged to become an authorized distributor of AbilityOne products. For more information on the AbilityOne Program and how to become an authorized distributor, please visit www.abilityone.gov. Point of contact at the AbilityOne Program is Mr. Eric Beale at ebeale@abilityone.gov or (703) 603-2119 *(current at the time of publication)*.

Becoming a successful FSS contractor requires that your company take a few key steps. The first step to success under the FSS Program is to perform due diligence and understand your commitments and obligations as an FSS contractor. Companies that have prepared well to understand their commitments and obligations, and have plans to meet those commitments and obligations, have thrived under the FSS Program.

The next step is to select the schedule that best aligns to the commercial supplies and/or services your company wants to offer. This action can be accomplished by accessing GSA eLibrary (formerly called, Schedules eLibrary) at www.gsaelibrary.gsa.gov. Under the "Schedules Contracts" box on the right, select "View Schedules Contracts" to view the complete list of schedules. By clicking on any schedule number, you can then view the generic categories of supplies and/or services under a particular schedule. For more information about GSA eLibrary, go to www.gsa.gov/elibrary. Detailed information on selecting the schedule(s) that best aligns to your offering can be found in the Vendor Toolbox.

Once you have determined the proper schedule under which to submit your offer, the next step is to download, read, and understand the solicitation. You may access this solicitation by clicking on "Vendors: Click here to view the current solicitation on FedBizOpps," which is located on each individual schedule's page. It is essential to read the entire schedule solicitation. Understanding the terms and conditions of an FSS contract and your contractual obligations is critical to your success as an FSS contract holder.

You can also download the solicitation directly from <u>FedBizOpps</u> by accessing www.fedbizopps.gov. From the FedBizOpps website, you may search by GSA Office, VA National Acquisition Center, Solicitation Number, or Keyword. We encourage you to visit both GSA eLibrary and FedBizOpps, since each site provides important news and information.

Please note that the award of an FSS contract does NOT guarantee future sales, and it is up to you to market your company. Although the FSS Program provides significant benefits to ordering activities, you are not required to use the FSS Program to fulfill their requirements. With thousands of contracts already in place, competition for orders under the FSS Program is fierce.

2. How to decide if a GSA/FSS Contract is right for you:

First, take the mandatory Pathway to Success free education seminar and test. Pathway to Success is designed to assist prospective GSA Schedule contractors in making informed business decisions as to whether obtaining a GSA Schedule contract is in their best interest. The presentation also provides background information on the GSA Schedules program. Pathway to Success is available online on the Vendor Support Center (VSC) website found at <u>https://vsc.gsa.gov</u>. Once on the VSC website, select "Pathway to Success" under the "Education" tab. Alternately, Pathway to Success can be found on the Vendor Education Center. Go to: <u>https://gsafas.secure.force.com/MASTrainingHome</u>. E-mail <u>pathwaytosuccess@gsa.gov</u> if you have questions related to the Pathway to Success training. The seminar includes topics such as expectations of vendors, how to compete and succeed as a schedule contractor, how to develop a schedule-specific business plan, and how to submit a quality offer.

Next, take the mandatory Readiness Assessment free self-evaluation. The Readiness Assessment is designed to assist prospective offerors in researching, analyzing, and deciding whether they are able to compete as an FSS contractor. The mandatory Readiness Assessment resides in the Vendor Toolbox on the Vendor Education Center, (<u>https://gsafas.secure.force.com/MASTrainingHome</u>), but can also be accessed through the VSC website under the "Education" tab. This tool will help your firm understand the amount of time and money that are needed to be a successful FSS contractor. It is required that this assessment be signed by an officer of your firm who is authorized to commit, and it is mandatory before submitting an offer. It is important that your firm understand the solicitation clauses and requirements such as past performance and certifications, etc. Therefore, it is suggested that an officer carefully read and review the solicitation to which your firm will be responding PRIOR to completing this assessment. The assessment contains a combination of "Yes/No" and short answer questions. Each question will reference a step in the Vendor Toolbox that will assist your firm in researching, analyzing, and deciding if you are ready to become an MAS contractor.

Next, locate the "New Contractor Orientation" webcast under the "Vendor Training" tab on the <u>Vendor Support Center (VSC)</u> website. The webcast was developed to define key contract requirements with which a vendor must comply, and outlines how GSA/VA evaluates FSS contract performance. While visiting the VSC, also review *The Steps to Success: Make the Most of your GSA Contract* under the "Publications" tab. This document provides an overview of FSS contract requirements including key reporting documents. Both learning tools are highly recommended reading, as they provide information for you to confidently comply with contractual obligations and ensure that you are ready to be an excellent FSS contractor. For more information about the VSC, visit <u>https://vsc.gsa.gov</u>.

Also, you can identify and assess your competition. This important task can be accomplished by visiting GSA eLibrary at: <u>http://www.gsaelibrary.gsa.gov/ElibMain/home.do</u> and <u>GSA Advantage!</u>® at <u>https://www.gsaadvantage.gov/advantage/main/start_page.do</u>. In addition to providing access to schedule solicitations, GSA eLibrary is the online source for FSS contract award information; GSA Advantage!® is the online shopping and ordering system. Both websites contain information regarding the supplies and/or services that current FSS contractors offer. The information collected from these websites should assist you in identifying potential competitors under the FSS Program. The knowledge gained from this effort will help you assess your firm's ability to compete, if awarded an FSS contract. Your review of the competition should include competitors' pricing, delivery times, warranty terms, services, and any other elements that make their offerings distinctive. For more information about GSA Advantage!®, visit: https://www.gsaadvantage.gov/advantage/main/start_page.do.

Another online tool for assessing your FSS Program competition is Schedule Sales Query (SSQ) at http://ssq.gsa.gov. SSQ provides detailed sales information on current FSS contractors. On this site, you can search to see if your competitors have successfully sold similar supplies and/or services under the FSS Program. For more information on SSQ, visit www.gsa.gov/schedulesalesquery.

Your review and analysis of the preceding websites should allow you to assess the competitive environment for the supplies and/or services you want to provide. Once you understand the requirements which you will have to follow, and the market in which you will have to operate, you can then decide whether an FSS contract is the right business investment for your firm.

I recommend you become familiar with the Federal PPE (Procurement Proposal Evaluation) factors. At a minimum, government buyers will evaluate price and past performance, and possibly your firm's expertise, in providing the supplies and/or services you are seeking to offer. Purchasers under the FSS Program make a selection of an FSS contractor based upon "best value." FAR 2.101 define "best value" as the expected outcome of an acquisition that, in the Government's estimation, provides the greatest overall benefit in response to the requirement.

Another important criteria to consider is whether the items you propose are compliant with the Trade Agreements Act, which can be found at: http://acquisition.gov/far/current/html/Subpart%2025_4.html#wp1086589. The Trade Agreements Act, (19 U.S.C. 2501, *et seq.*), is the enabling statute that implements numerous multi-lateral and bi-lateral international trade agreements and other trade initiatives. Since the estimated dollar value of each schedule exceeds the established Trade Agreements Act (TAA) threshold, the TAA is applicable to all schedules. In accordance with the TAA, only U.S.-made or designated country end products shall be offered and sold under schedule contracts. For the definition of "designated country," go to: http://acquisition.gov/far/current/html/Subpart%2025_1.html#wp1118780.

GSA offers ordering activity buyer's training and provides them with informational material about the benefits of the FSS Program. Such benefits include the following:

- Acquisition lead time is reduced;
- A wide selection of state-of-the-art commercial supplies and/or services;
- Schedule orders are not required to be synopsized;
- GSA has already determined schedule prices to be fair and reasonable.

Although GSA/VA provides informational material on the benefits of the FSS Program, GSA/VA does not market or promote specific contracts, distribute products of individual firms, or steer business to any individual contractor. If awarded an FSS contract, you will be required to market your supplies and/or services to ordering activities. You will be required to upload an approved schedule price list on GSA Advantage!®. Since purchasing authority is spread out across all ordering activities, marketing your supplies and/or services may not be an easy task. You are strongly encouraged to target markets and build relationships in much the same way you market to commercial customers. Finally, how well you perform under your FSS contract is up to you.

If you decide to submit an offer and are awarded an FSS contract, be advised that GSA will require your sales to exceed $25,000 within the first 24 months after your contract is awarded. Your company will then be expected to exceed $25,000 in sales each succeeding 12-month period in order to retain your FSS contract. If your company is newly established, or has had low sales in the supplies and/or services you want to offer under the FSS Program, you should consider the difficulty you may have in meeting this performance requirement. If you ultimately decide to submit an offer under the FSS Program, having a business plan to meet this performance requirement will be critical to ensuring your success as an FSS contractor.

3. Yes, I want to submit an offer:

Once you have decided to submit an offer with GSA, this is the final step in the procurement process. GSA/VA is always looking for highly qualified firms to increase competition and serve the needs of the ordering activities. While not all firms are awarded FSS contracts, the FSS Program, in accordance with statutory authority, is open to all responsible offerors. To be considered for award of an FSS contract, you must demonstrate that your firm meets all FSS Program requirements including a reasonable and competitive price. To understand the term "responsible," please refer to FAR 9.104-1 which identifies the standards a prospective contractor must possess to be determined responsible. To read FAR 9.104-1, go to: http://acquisition.gov/far/current/html/Subpart%209_1. html#wp1084076.

Currently, the time required to evaluate and award an FSS contract can range from three to six months. Well-prepared and documented offers with competitive pricing are easier to evaluate and may expedite the award process.

GSA has developed eOffer, a web-based application that allows an offeror to prepare and submit an FSS offer electronically. eOffer is designed to create an interactive, secure environment that simplifies the contracting process from submission of offer to contract award. eOffer uses the latest digital authentication technology to ensure the integrity of data and to electronically sign the offer. Digital certificates are required in order to use eOffer. The eOffer website, at http://eoffer.gsa.gov, contains a variety of information regarding the eOffer application, including available training and information regarding digital certificates. It is required that eOffer be used to submit an offer. For more information on eOffer, visit www. gsa.gov/eoffer.

Once you submit an offer, the Procurement Contracting Officer (PCO) will look for a number of items. It will verify that you have submitted all the required information necessary to evaluate your offer. The following are key elements of your offer that will be reviewed:

- Pricing,
- Past performance,

- Scope -- the supplies/services are within the scope of the Schedule solicitation,
- Financial capability,
- Technical capability,
- Subcontracting Plan (if you are not a small business concern),
- Other regulatory compliance.

GSA, as well as Cal Stevens, want you to be successful. Therefore, every effort has been made to provide your firm with this helpful and useful information in seeking federal procurement opportunities.

4. No, I do not want to submit an offer right now. What other options do I have for federal business?

If you decide a FSS contract is not a good fit for your firm at this time, you can still participate in other Federal Government acquisitions. In some cases, pursuing other avenues may be even more advantageous.

Other government contracting opportunities are posted on FedBizOpps at www.fedbizopps.gov. Commercial vendors seeking federal markets can search, monitor, and retrieve solicitations for supplies and services issued by all federal agencies. The FAR addresses the circumstances under which an acquisition of supplies and/or services with an estimated dollar value exceeding $3,000, but not over the simplified acquisition threshold, gives preference to small business concerns.

Business concerns may also participate in subcontracting opportunities with companies already under contract to the Federal Government. The U.S. Small Business Administration (www.sba.gov) provides information on subcontracting, as well as other topics of interest, to firms seeking business opportunities. Existing schedule contractors are always looking for opportunities to subcontract to small business, small disadvantaged business, women-owned small business, HUBZone small business, veteran-owned small business, and service-disabled veteran-owned small business concerns.

Remember, the FSS Program is continually open. If you have determined the FSS Program is not the correct contracting vehicle for your firm at this time, GSA encourages you to periodically revisit your business plan and the opportunity to market your supplies and/or services under the FSS Program at a later date.

I hope this information will assist your company in implementing your tactical plans in taking the time to learn about the FSS Program. Uncle Sam wishes you great success in whatever method you choose to market to government agencies.

Finally, how well you perform under the contract is the most critical element of your success! Implementing, and then executing, your tactical plans will assist your efforts in becoming a successful contractor to Uncle Sam.

End Notes:

Chapter Five – Final Thoughts

There is an old saying, "If you want to succeed - prepare well!" This saying not only applies to real life situations, but business or economic situations. It is also said that small businesses drive the economy. Well, if that's true, the economy is in trouble, because small businesses are struggling in today's economy. However, there is always light at the end of the tunnel. There are opportunities for small businesses to succeed. The U.S. Small Business Administration and other governmental agencies, a.k.a. Uncle Sam, need to step up to the plate and be true advocates for small businesses in the government procurement arena.

There are small business set asides, i.e., Service Disabled Veteran-Owned Business, Small Disadvantaged, and other social economical programs that are not being utilized to the full extent practical. Federal, and in some cases, state and local buyers, would rather do business with large corporations, (and there is nothing wrong with doing business with large corporations), rather than provide opportunities for small businesses because of the unfounded fear that the small business(es) would not do a satisfactory job. Although GSA Multiple Award Schedule (MAS) or Federal Supply Schedule (FSS) contracts have been awarded to small businesses, 80% vs. 20%, many believe (I am one of them), that Uncle Sam, including GSA, can do more to offer true procurement opportunities to small businesses. Here's another interesting fact.

When "the rubber meets the road," small businesses receive approximately 40% of the task or delivery orders (check www.fedbizopps.gov and **Government Executive Magazine**).

The point is… "Any enterprise built by wise planning, becomes strong."-- *Proverbs* 24:3. So then what happens when you're not well-prepared? Things you hope won't happen, do, and they occur with greater frequency than the things you hope will happen. The dividing line between winning and losing is preparation! The late tennis champion Arthur Ashe said, "The key to winning is self-confidence, and the key to self-confidence is preparation." Singing, "If You Wish Upon a Star" won't make your dreams come true; you've got to prepare yourself.

In a biblical sense, ever wonder what Jesus was doing during those pre-dawn risings and nights of prayer? Preparing! If you plan to keep growing, preparation must become a way of life. You must never stop asking, "Lord, what do you want me to do?" What will it cost me in time, effort, and resources? What obstacles must I overcome?" If you live with that mindset, you'll be well on your way to fulfilling God's purpose for your life and the success of your company.

You've got to educate yourself and your key associates if you want to be successful in obtaining contracts and marketing to Uncle Sam. This is one of many published books and topics on this subject. Continue to read informational books. Attend small business outreach events whenever possible. Network with organizations that are advocates for small businesses. Seek change in encouraging federal buyers, civilian, and military agencies to offer more procurement opportunities to the small business community. You have to be an advocate for change and be ready to fulfill the responsibility that goes with those changes.

Asked how long it would take to bring his ship to a stop, the Queen Mary's captain replied, "A little over a mile." Then he added, "A good captain thinks at least a mile ahead." Your success in any venture, including obtaining government contracts from Uncle Sam, is determined by how important it is to you and your ability to prepare for it. **The Living Bible** paraphrases it this way: "Any enterprise that is built by wise planning becomes strong through common sense, and profits wonderfully by keeping abreast of the facts." Alexander Hamilton, a founding father of the United States, said, "Men give me credit for genius, but all the genius I have lies in this: when I have a subject to hand, I study it profoundly." So, if you want to succeed – prepare.

Finally, I hope I've inspired small (and mid-size) businesses to seek procurement opportunities with Uncle Sam. The economy will be thankful and so will your business. Best wishes in your efforts to seek procurement opportunities, and may God bless all your future endeavors!

Chapter Six –Resources

Selected Web Sites for Small Businesses

GSA's Website   www.gsa.gov

GSA's Native American Business Center   www.gsa.gov/nabc
     GSA's national office assisting Native   www.gsa.gov/itn
     Americans/Alaska Natives

GSA's Office of Small Business Utilization Center   www.gsa.gov/sbuc
     ** Forecast of Contracting Opportunities
     Subcontracting Directory
     Click on Doing Business with GSA booklet
     under "Publication"

GSA's Federal Acquisition Service (FAS)   www.gsa.gov/fss
     GSA Advantage
     Federal Supply Schedule – what is it?
     Schedules e-Library – how to access
     E-Buy – how to access
     Contract offers and contract modifications   http://eoffer.gsa.gov
     GSA's Fleet Management   www.gsa.gov/vehicle
     Vehicle Acquisition & Leasing Services
     Technology Contracts
     Information Technology
     Professional Services

GSA's Public Buildings Service (PBS)   www.gsa.gov/pbs

    Real Property Asset Management

    Chief Architect

    Inventory of Owned & Leased Properties

    Real Estate Services

    Real Estate Disposal

MARKETING TOOLS

Office of Small Business Utilization (OSBU)

    OSBU's Subcontracting Directory   http://w3.gsa.gov/web/i/ subs_dir.nsf

    OSBU's Forecast of Contracting   http://w3.gsa.gov/web/i/ ion/con_opp.nsf

Federal Procurement Data Report – New   www.fpds-ng.com
Generation (FPDS-NG)

Department of Defense   www.acq.ods.mil/sadbu

    Small & Disadvantaged Business Utilization
    Office

Federal Agencies on the Internet   www.lib.lsu.edu/gov/ fedgov.html

List of Excluded Parties   http://epls.arnet.gov

CONTRACT OPPORTUNITIES

FedBizOpps   www.fedbizopps.gov

E-Buy   www.ebuy.gsa.gov

Federal Acquisition Jump station   http://nais.nasa.gov/ fedproc/home.html

Department of Defense Business Opportunities   www.dla.mil
"Business opportunities"

RESOURCES

Electronic Government   http://egov.gov

Center for Veterans' Enterprise   www.vetbiz.gov

Small Business Administration   www.sba.gov
    HUBZone Certification
    8(a) Program Certification
    Service Disabled Veteran Owned Business
    Other Small Business Programs/Resources
Procurement Technical Assistance Centers   www.dla.mil/db/procurem.htm

Federal Marketplace – Procurement Resource   www.fedmarket.com
Gateway Writing Business Plans
Consumer Information Center   www.pueblo.gsa.gov
Index of Government Information   www.fedworld.gov
Catalog of Federal Domestic Assistance   www.cfda.gov
One Stop Online Access to Grants   www.grants.gov
Government Wide Information   www.firstgov.gov
United Indian Development Association   www.uida.org
National Conference for American Indian   www.ncaied.org
Economic Development

TO DO CHECK LIST FOR SMALL BUSINESSES

FedBizOpps Electronic Posting System   www.fedbizopps.gov
System for Award Management (SAM)   www.SAM.gov
Dun & Bradstreet (DUNS Number)   www.dnb.com
North American Industry Classification (NAICS)   www.census.gov click on "NAICS" or www.naics.com/index.html

Business Partner Network (ORCA)   www.bpn.gov
Information Technology businesses only   http://it-solutions.gsa.gov
Small Business certifications   www.sba.gov

GENERAL INFORMATION

Department of Labor   www.wdol.gov
    On line Wage Determinations
    Service Contract Act (SCA) & Davis-Bacon
    Act (DBA)

Federal Acquisition Regulation (FAR)   www.arnet.gov/far

Code of Federal Regulations (CFAR)   www.gpoaccess.gov/cfr/
index.html

DEFINITIONS:

Special Item Number (SIN)

Contractor and Government Entity Code
(CAGE code)

GENERAL PUBLICATIONS

Federal Times Newspaper   www.federaltimes.com

Government Executive Magazine   www.govexec.com

American Society for Quality   www.asq.org

National Contract Management Association   www.ncmahq.org

Appendix A –
Selected Websites for Small Businesses

OTHER PROCUREMENT SITES

U.S. Air Force :
http://www.af.mil/sites/

Air Force Long Range Acquisition Estimate Procurement Forecast:
http://www.selltoairforce.org/Opportunities/af-query.asp

Air Force Contracting Reports:
http://www.safaq.hq.af.mil/contracting/reporting/

U.S. Navy:
http://www.abm.rda.hq.navy.mil/navyoas/content/view/full/187

DoD Procurement Reports:
http://www.siadapp.dior.whs.mil/procurement/Procurement.html

U.S. Army Corps of Engineers:
http://www.usace.army.mil/where.html

U.S. Department of Agriculture Procurement Forecast:
http://www.pforecast.net/index.html

U.S. Department of Energy:
http://www.safaq.hq.af.mil/contracting/reproting/

U.S. Environmental Protection Agency:
http://www.yosemite1.epa.gov/oarm/oam/forecastdatabase.nsf

U.S. Housing & Urban Development   :
http://www.hud.gov/offices/cpo/contracts.cfm

U.S. Department of Interior:
http://www.ideasec.nbc.gov/forecast

U.S. Department of Justice:
http://www.usdoj.gov/07business/07_5.html

National Aeronautics & Space Administration- Johnson Space Center:
http://procurement.jsc.nasa.gov/jscaf.htm

U.S. Department of Transportation:
http://www.osdbuweb.dot.gov/osdbu_servcies/Procruement/forceast.cfm

U. S. Department of Treasury
http://www.ustreas.gov/offices/management/dcfo/osdbu/marketing-publications/forecast.shtml

U.S. Department of Veterans Affairs:
http://www.bos.oamm.va.gov/cgi-bin/WebObjects/FcoPublic.woa

Procurement Technical Assistance Centers Listing:
http://www.dla.mil/db/procurem.htm

NOTE: Current as the date of publication.

(AUTHOR'S NOTE: List any website here during your research, if not listed above)

Appendix B –
Top 10 GSA Schedules in Fiscal Year 2013

IT Schedule 70 is the dominant General Services Administration (GSA) Schedule by sales, accounting for more than 40% of 2013 volume. MOBIS, a management and professional services program, was second.

GSA Schedule 2013 Sales:

Schedule	FY 2013 Sales
1. 70: Information Technology	$14,434,856,538
2. 874: MOBIS	$4,445,445,865
3. 871: Professional Engineering Services	$2,801,631,367
4. 84: Law Enforcement	$2,011,629,701
5. 520: Financial and Business Solutions	$1,914,127,170
6. 71: Furniture	$1,036,485,420
7. CORP	$808,532,883
8. 36: Office, Imaging, and Document Solution	$723,454,615
9. 874 V: Logistics Worldwide	$669,104,160
10. 66: Scientific Equipment and Services	$656,707,103

Source: 2013 Annual Review of Government Contracting by National Contract Management Association and Bloomberg Government

Appendix C – Common Terms

Blanket Purchase Agreements (BPAs) – BPAs are contracts that set standard prices and terms for products and services that are commonly ordered by an agency. By creating BPAs, an agency can leverage its combined buying power to take advantage of quantity discounts. Because vendors compete for the BPA when it is established, competition is not required for individual purchases from a BPA, which saves agencies administrative time and money.

System for Award Management (SAM) – The SAM is the primary vendor database for the federal government. Both current and potential government vendors are required to register in SAM in order to be awarded contracts by the government. Note, to register with the SAM, you must first obtain a DUNS number.

Dun and Bradstreet Universal Numbering System (DUNS) – DUNS provides a unique nine-digit identification number for each physical location of a business. A DUNS number is required to register in the CCR and is free for all businesses required to do so.

Employer Identification Number (EIN) – An EIN serves as the Taxpayer Identification Number (TIN) for businesses. In short, it is a business's version of a Social Security Number. EINs may be requested from the Internal Revenue Service.

Federal Prisons Industries, Inc. (FPI) – The Federal Prisons Industries, also known as UNICOR, employs and provides skill training to federal inmates who produce market-price quality goods for sale to the federal government. UNICOR's mission is to contribute to the safety and security of correctional facilities by keeping inmates constructively occupied, operate in a self-sustaining manner, and minimize FPI's impact on private business and labor.

GSA (U.S. General Services Administration) Schedules – GSA Schedules are long-term government-wide contracts that establish set prices and terms for supplies and services. Because ordering from these established contracts saves government agencies administrative time and money, preference is often given to vendors on a GSA Schedule. Businesses interested in becoming a GSA Schedule contractor should visit GSA's site for vendors. GSA Schedules are also referred to as Multiple Award Schedules and Federal Supply Schedules.

HUBZone – The HUBZone Program stimulates economic development and creates jobs in urban and rural communities by providing federal contracting preferences to HUBZone small businesses. HUBZone (Historically Underutilized Business Zone) certification requires that a business employ staff who lives in a HUBZone and maintains a "principal office" in a HUBZone. The program resulted from provisions contained in the Small Business Reauthorization Act of 1997.

JWOD Participating Nonprofit Agencies – JWOD participating nonprofit agencies employ people who are blind or have other severe disabilities. The Javits-Wagner-O'Day (JWOD) Act requires that federal agencies procure certain items and services from these agencies. The JWOD Act also established the Committee for Purchase from People Who Are Blind or Severely Disabled, which is an independent government activity responsible for determining which supplies and services must be purchased from JWOD agencies, establishing prices for the supplies and services, and establishing rules and regulations to implement the JWOD Act.

North American Industry Classification System (NAICS) – NAICS is a six-digit hierarchical coding system to classify all economic activity into twenty industry sectors. NAICS replaced the U.S. Standard Industrial Classification (SIC) system in October 2000.

Online Representations and Certifications Application (ORCA) – ORCA is an e-government initiative that replaces most of the paper based Representations and Certifications (Reps and Certs) process, known as Section K.

Service-Disabled Veteran-Owned (SDVO) Small Business – A SDVO small business must be at least 51 percent unconditionally and directly owned by one or more service-disabled veterans. This can include a publicly owned business that has at least 51 percent of its stock unconditionally owned by one or more service-disabled veterans. The management and daily business operations of the SDVO small business must be controlled by one or more service-disabled veterans (or in the case of a veteran with permanent and severe disability, the spouse or permanent caregiver of such veteran). A SDVO small business may self-certify in the System for Awards Management.

Small Business – The definition of a small business varies by industry. The Small Business Administration provides information on these "size standards" by industry.

Small Disadvantaged Business (SDB) – SBDs are small businesses that are at least 51 percent owned by one or more individuals who are both socially and economically disadvantaged. This can include publicly owned businesses that have at least 51 percent of stock unconditionally owned by one or more socially and economically disadvantaged individuals and whose management and daily business is controlled by one or more such individuals. 8(a) firms automatically qualify for SDB certification.

Taxpayer Identification Number (TIN) – A TIN is a nine-digit number used for tax processing. An individual's TIN is his/her Social Security Number (SSN), and a business's TIN is its Employer Identifying Number (EIN).

Women-Owned Small Business – Women-owned small businesses may self-certify in the Systems for Awards Management.

TACADA
MARKETING
We Are Your Partners for Success

P.O. BOX 373855
DECATUR, GA 30037-3855
404.288.3604

Capability Statement

DUNS: 027770598
System for Award Management (SAM) Registration
(formerly CCR & ORCA): Current and Active
NAICS: 541611, 541612, 541613, 611430
SIC: 7389, 8742, 8748, 8299
Registration: Small Veteran-Owned Business

Who We Are

TACADA Marketing Consultants, LLC, is a veteran-owned, small, consulting and professional development and training company. We offer cost effective, enterprise-wide professional development solutions delivered by experienced professionals with many years of business, government, industry, and human resources knowledge and expertise. Its president and founder, Calvin Stevens, is a General Services Administration (GSA) retiree with over 30 years of contracting, management, marketing and quality assurance experience. He has considerable knowledge on marketing to federal and military agencies.

Background

TACADA Marketing Consultants was founded in 1998 as a "part-time" professional development and training firm, offering hands-on, results-oriented training in such subjects as interviewing skills, resume writing, and professional development and coaching. Its training programs were geared primarily to federal and military employees who lacked the needed competencies to further enhance their professional development. Over the years, TACADA has trained thousands of employees of government agencies and private corporations in enhancing the career and professional development of its employees. In 2009, TACADA went "full-time" and entered the small business consultant and training arena based on Calvin's 34 years of counseling, coaching, contracting, and marketing experience with GSA and the Air Force Reserves.

Our Competencies

- Professional development workshops and seminars geared to enhancing career development and assisting employees in reaching their full potential
    - Building Trust
    - Communicating Effectively
    - Networking
    - Partnering
- Results-oriented consultant services to small businesses seeking to do business with and how to market their products and services to federal, state, and local governments.
    - Analyzing Needs
    - Proposing Solutions
    - Applying Procurement Skills
    - Applying Marketing Skills
    - Driving Results

Services

TACADA Marketing will provide consultation service in the following areas:

1. How to obtain a General Services Administration (GSA) schedule contract
2. How to market your products and services to federal and military agencies
3. How to develop employees to enhance productivity and professional development

Government and military agencies, non-profit organizations, and corporate human resources offices, have the ability to leverage the experience and expertise in developing and providing training opportunities to their employees for career enhancement and job satisfaction. Small businesses have access to an experienced former government professional in identifying, analyzing and seeking procurement and marketing opportunities with federal, military, and state and local government entities.

A one-hour consultation will include a review of your strategic and tactical plans.

For more information:

Visit http://www.tacadamarketing.com

Call 404.275.2386
president@tacadamarketing.com

You Can Sell to Uncle Sam

It takes tenacity to succeed in government sales or to sell your products or services to "Uncle Sam." Establishing a small business in the federal marketplace can be frustrating. Yet, small business preference programs, along with knowledge of how procurements are conducted, can cause a small business to grow to over $1 million dollars in revenue in a few short years.

A General Services Administration (GSA) Contract or Multiple Award Schedule is a pre-approved contract to do business with the government. Becoming a GSA Schedule holder deems you worthy of federal business; your prices have been determined to be fair and reasonable, and your competency in your field has been given a stamp of approval. Government buyers know you are not a risky prospect and can make purchases from you, directly with you, or through GSA Advantage (the government's online shopping mall), or with any government purchase card (GSA contracts permit the use of government credit card purchases). Billions of dollars are spent each fiscal year through GSA contracts by civilian and military agencies. A GSA Schedule contract is attractive to both buyer and seller; it's a win - win situation. This book will provide guidance on how your company can position itself in selling its products or services to Uncle Sam.

About the Author

Cal Stevens, President, TACADA Marketing Consultants, LLC, author and consultant to small businesses and professional development trainer, retired from GSA after 30 years of service. Cal served in various leadership positions in GSA and has developed competencies in contracting, contract administration, marketing, warehouse distribution and quality assurance. Cal is devoting his efforts to assisting small businesses in obtaining government contracts and how to market to civilian and military agencies.

"Having TACADA Marketing—specifically Cal Stevens, consult us at Contract Business Interiors, Inc. on getting a GSA Schedule has been a great business decision. Acquiring a schedule is a complicated process. Cal's years of experience in GSA gives him first-hand knowledge of the process and the best… and quickest… way to succeed. Cal also provides usable information on marketing opportunities related to our scope of work. I frequently receive interesting articles and notices of events that can help how I do business at CBI. In my view, he's the expert and I trust what he says." --- Quentin Bradford, Account Manager, Contract Business Interiors, Inc.

"Cal Stevens has been an invaluable resource for me in my fifteen years as a Small Business Advocate specializing in opening doors in the Federal procurement maze for small business owners. Cal's vast depth of procurement knowledge coupled with his professionalism and cheerful nature made him my, 'Go to Guy.' For simple and complex procurement problems. Read this book, 'You Can Sell to Uncle Sam' for businesses interested in federal procurement." --- Dave Gibson, Small Business Advocate, Public Buildings Service, GSA.

For additional information, visit: **www.TACADAMarketing.com**

www.ingramcontent.com/pod-product-compliance
Lightning Source LLC
Chambersburg PA
CBHW021025180526
45163CB00005B/2118